GW00672421

En-
chant-
ing
Ticino

Acknowledgements

Sig.ra Daniela Solcà, studio for string instruments, Mendrisio
Sig. Carlo Fontana, Castel San Pietro
Sig. Paolo Selldorf, Dipl. Ing. ETH, Incinerator (ACR) Giubiasco
Sig. Rudolf Stockar, Geologist and Paleontologist, Natural History Museum Lugano
Sig. Gabriele Schrag, Delea winery
Sig. Gampiero Ferrazzini, President of "Società Navigazione Lago di Lugano"
Sig. Ernesto Merz, Balloon Team SA, Lugano
Arch. Marino Venturini, Chocolate Factory Cima Norma, Dangio
Perseo Foundry, Mendrisio
The management of «Teatro Dimitri», Verscio

With special thanks to:
my husband Juliusz for his support and never ending patience

also to:
Mervyn Hills
Iwo Zaluski
Sandra Parkinson

and John Arthur who inspired this book

STAMPATO IN TICINO

Designed and produced by
Salvioni arti grafiche, Bellinzona

Printed in December 2011

ISBN 978-88-7967-268-9

Enchanting Ticino

Photographs by
Hanna Komarnicki

Text by
Hanna and
Juliusz Komarnicki

SalvioniEdizioni

Enchanting Ticino

Ticino is the most southerly canton of Switzerland and extends from the Gotthard massif down to Bellinzona, Lake Maggiore and the Locarno region and also to the area of Lake Lugano. The climate largely mirrors this diverse geography, ranging from the cool alpine altitudes to balmy valley breezes and a subtropical climate near the lakes in the south. Ticino is often referred to as the «Riviera of Switzerland».

Like other cantons, sovereign states within the Swiss Confederation, Ticino also has its own parliament and judiciary. The official language is Italian and the inhabitants are strongly influenced by the lifestyle of Italy, which lies immediately to the south. As has been the case elsewhere in Switzerland, Ticino has had a violent history. Parts of the present canton were at one time subject to Italian dominance before being conquered by Swiss cantons to the north. Ticino, as it is today, became part of Switzerland in 1803.

For many centuries the region suffered great hardship. As a result, the population was forced to become industrious and resourceful to be able to exist. The cultural heritage which survives from that time gives a glimpse into a past which is of great interest. However, from the 19th century onwards, once the pass over the Gotthard had been improved and the present rail and road tunnels built, the area florished at a rapid pace and is now notably prosperous.

Ticino is easily reached by road, train and air, due to the international airport near Lugano. This well situated canton offers every level of comfort and luxury in an ideal setting. Any traveller, sportsman, tourist, businessman or anyone just looking for somewhere to relax and enjoy good food and good wine in a southern atmosphere need look no further. The landscape of lakes, startling cascades, inviting rivers, forests and snowy peaks lends itself to a wide range of excursions where a good road system with excellent postal bus services and plentiful cableways provide convenient access. A long tradition of stonemasonry and of both rural and contemporary architecture in Ticino has ensured that there is plenty to discover in the towns and villages. Is it just the extraordinary light which has inspired so many painters, writers, poets and philosophers?

The Ticino River, which lends its name to the canton, has its sources in the northern Gotthard massif, an important water shed. It rushes south along the valleys, passing numerous villages on the way to Bellinzona, the capital of the canton, which boasts three splendid medieval castles, all UNESCO World Heritage Listed (WHL) protected sites. The valley widens as the river flows through the fertile plain of Magadino, before gently spreading out into a delta surrounded by a nature reserve. At this point the river enters Lake Maggiore, where many attractive places are situated. Locarno and its smaller sister Ascona and finally Brissago and its islands offer a particularly southern atmosphere. There are also numerous delightful individual villages and valleys of unforgettable scenery.

In the south-east the land slopes down to Lake Lugano and continues all the way to the border with Italy at Chiasso, an important frontier town. Within this area lies Lugano, not only the pre-eminent centre for financial services but also an important cultural hub. Built around the bay of Lake Lugano it is flanked by two mountains, Monte San Salvatore and Monte Bré which give the city its characteristic skyline. Picturesque areas in the vicinity, such as the «Malcantone» attract both locals and visitors. Mendrisio, a beauty spot in itself, also has a nearby industrial area and shopping centres. This is also the region of Monte San Giorgio, famous for its fossils (UNESCO WHL) and of Monte Generoso with its rack railway; both are well worth visiting.

Economically Ticino has become a leading centre in Switzerland for financial services and banking. Many entrepreneurs have developed flourishing businesses, where Swiss precision is combined with Italian flair. It has also attracted a multitude of well established international companies that have their headquarters or their logistical centres in this canton.

Academically Ticino has prominent international private colleges and a university situated in Lugano, with its renowned faculty of architecture in Mendrisio. Important research centres have attracted numerous scientists from all over the world.

For those who like shopping, Ticino provides a variety of opportunities. Markets of all kinds can be explored in most towns or villages, but also shopping centres, department stores and fashion boutiques tempt the eye.

Throughout the year there is no lack of cultural events: art exhibitions, concerts and performances of all kinds, hosting world famous personalities. In the summer well known music festivals and the much appreciated Locarno Film Festival complete the very wide choice.

In the pictures that follow, the author hopes to give a glimpse of the activities, buildings and geography of the canton, in many of them you will notice the four elements; earth, air, fire and water. Ticino has all of them.

Index

Upper Ticino
and lake Maggiore area

15

CACAO
SANTÉ
Cima
DANGIO
SUISSE

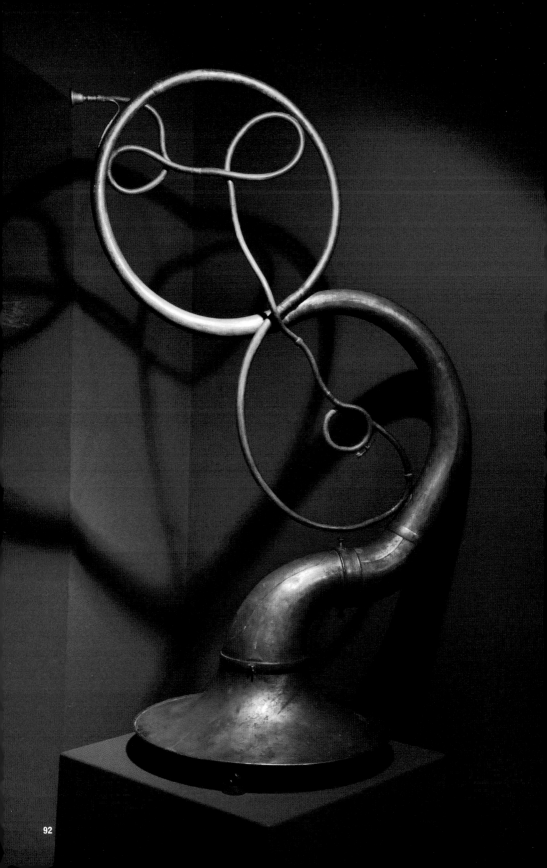

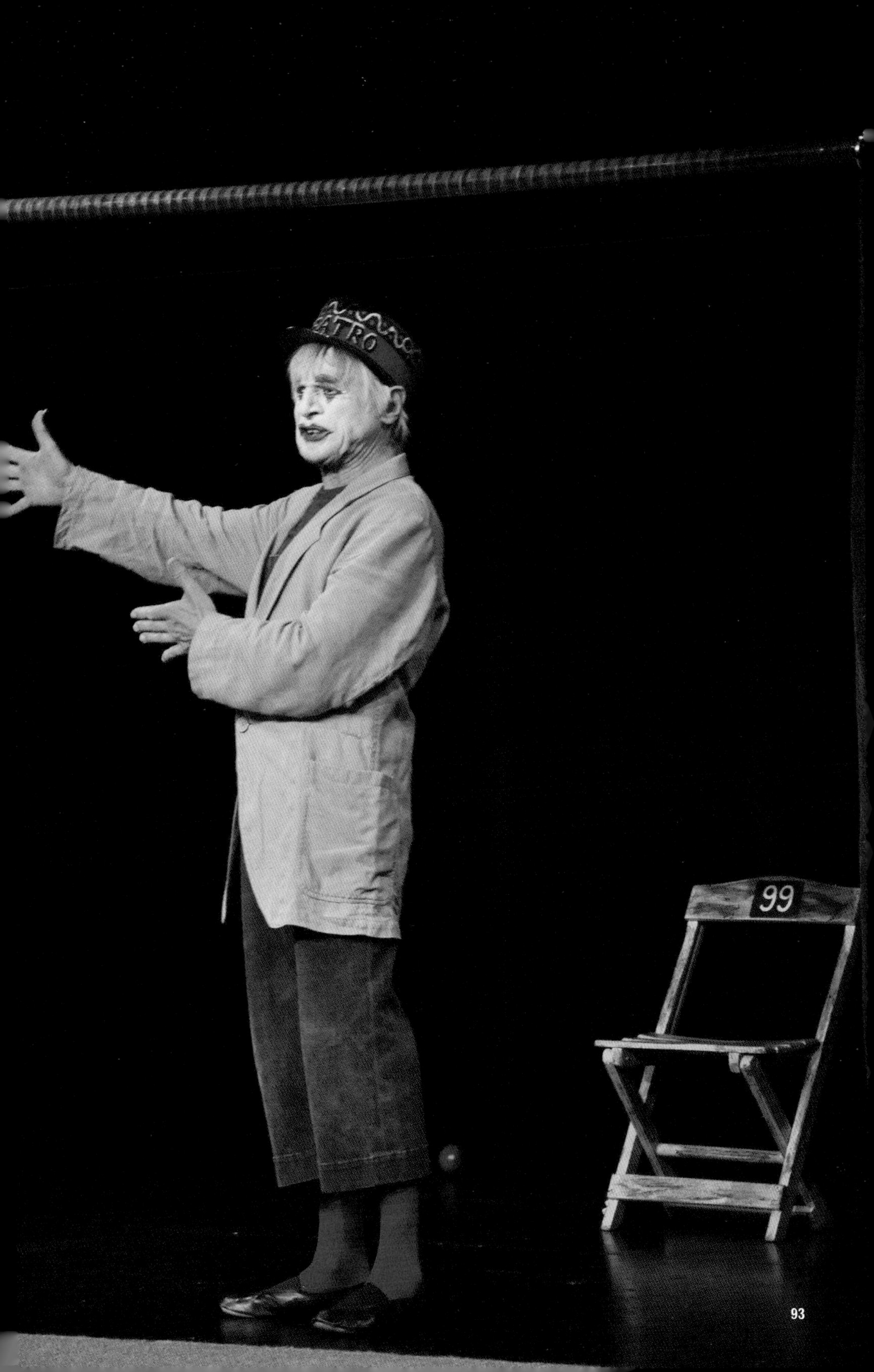
99

Lower Ticino
including lake Lugano area

139

SALUMERIA

Gabbani
LO SHOPPING

Sprite
33 cl. CHF 2.50
Fanta
33 cl. CHF 2.50
Coca Cola light
33 cl. CHF 2.50
Coca Cola
33 cl. CHF 2.50
Acqua minerale
33 cl. CHF 2.50
Thè al limone
25 cl. CHF 2.50
Thè alla pesca
25 cl. CHF 2.50
Thè al limone
5 cl. CHF 3.50
Thè alla pesca
5 cl. CHF 3.50
Coca Cola
5 cl. CHF 3.50
Acqua minerale
5 cl. CHF 3.50
Birra
33 cl. CHF 3.50

Gabbani
LO SHOPPING

Sprite
33 cl. CHF 2.50
Fanta
33 cl. CHF 2.50
Coca Cola light
33 cl. CHF 2.50
Coca Cola
33 cl. CHF 2.50
Acqua minerale
33 cl. CHF 2.50
Thè al limone
25 cl. CHF 2.50
Thè alla pesca
25 cl. CHF 2.50
Thè al limone
5 cl. CHF 3.50
Coca Cola
5 cl. CHF 3.50
Acqua minerale
5 cl. CHF 3.50
Birra
33 cl. CHF 3.50

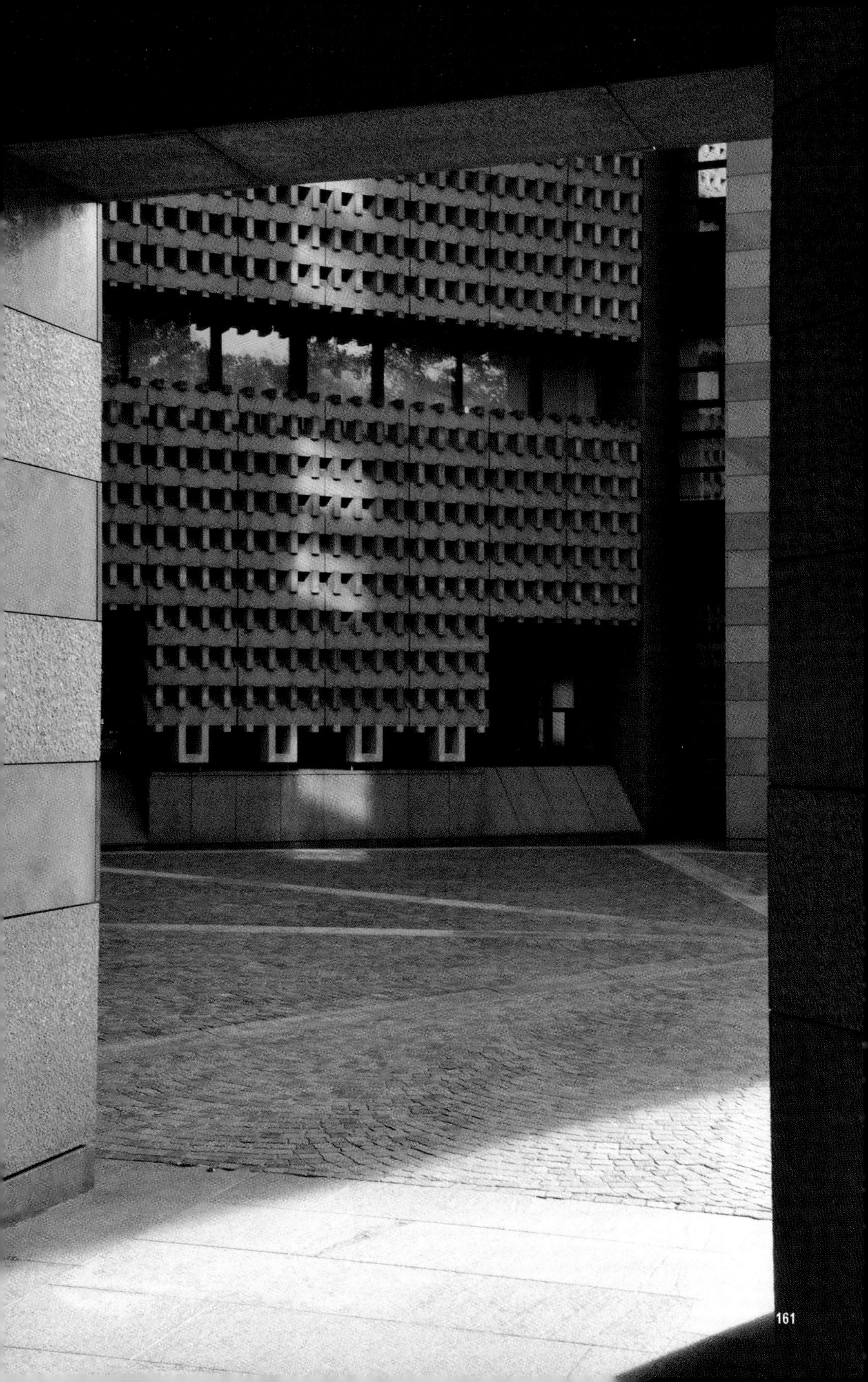

Palazzo Turconi

Accademia di architettura

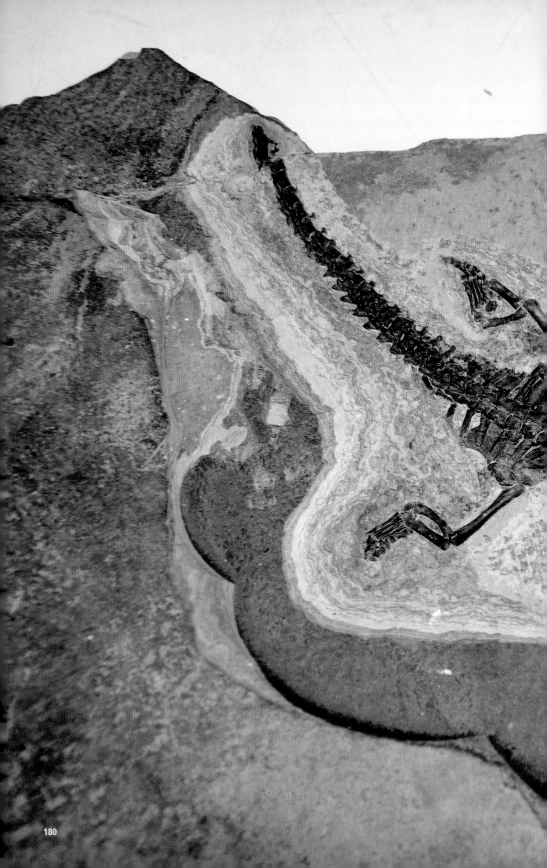

Some useful websites concerning Ticino

- www.ticino.ch

- www.bellinzonaturismo.ch

- www.luganoturismo.ch

- www.tio.ch

- www.myswitzerland.com

- www.mendrisiottoturismo.ch

- www.ascona-locarno.com

- Locarno Film Festival:

- www.pardo.ch

- www.youtube.com/user/ticinoturismo

- Financial matters:
  http://www.swissnetwork.com/topic-search/show/article/10211-doing-business-
  and-investments-in-ticino-attractiveness-and-role/

- Hotels:
  www.booking/region/ch/ticino